CLAMBAKE

WE ARE STILL HERE
NATIVE AMERICANS TODAY

A Wampanoag Tradition

Russell M. Peters
Photographs by John Madama
With a Foreword by Michael Dorris

Lerner Publications Company ● Minneapolis

Series Editor: Gordon Regguinti
Series Consultants: W. Roger Buffalohead, Juanita G. Corbine Espinosa
Illustrations by Carly Bordeau.

This book is available in two editions:
Library binding by Lerner Publications Company
Soft cover by First Avenue Editions
241 First Avenue North
Minneapolis, MN 55401

ISBN: 0-8225-2651-4 (lib. bdg.)
ISBN: 0-8225-9621-0 (pbk.)

LIBRARY OF CONGRESS CATALOGING-IN-PUBLICATION DATA

Peters, Russell M.
    Clambake—a Wampanoag tradition / Russell M. Peters ; photographs
by John Madama; foreword by Michael Dorris.
        p.   cm. — (We are still here)
    Includes bibliographical references.
    Summary: Steven Peters, a twelve-year-old Wampanoag Indian in
Massachusetts, learns from his grandfather how to prepare a clambake
in the tradition of his people.
    ISBN 0-8225-2651-4
    1. Wampanoag Indians—Rites and ceremonies—Juvenile literature.
2. Clambakes—Massachusetts—Mashpee—Juvenile literature.
3. Wampanoag Indians—Social life and customs—Juvenile literature.
[1. Wampanoag Indians—Rites and ceremonies. 2. Indians of North
America—Massachusetts—Rites and ceremonies. 3. Clambakes.
4. Peters, Steven.] I. Madama, John, ill. II. Title.
III. Series.
E99.W2P47   1992   92-8423
974.4'82—dc20   CIP
                                                     AC

Manufactured in the United States of America

1 2 3 4 5 6 97 96 95 94 93 92

To Amanda and my grandchildren

Foreword

by Michael Dorris

How do we get to be who we are? What are the ingredients that shape our values, customs, language, and tastes, that bond us into a unit different from any other? On a large scale, what makes the Swedes Swedish or the Japanese Japanese?

These questions become even more subtle and interesting when they're addressed to distinct and enduring traditional cultures coexisting within the boundaries of a large and complex society. Certainly Americans visiting abroad have no trouble recognizing their fellow countrymen and women, be they black or white, descended from Mexican or Polish ancestors, rich or poor. As a people, we have much in common, a great deal that we more or less share: a recent history, a language, a common denominator of popular music, entertainment, and politics.

But, if we are fortunate, we also belong to a small, more particular community, defined by ethnicity or kinship, belief system or geography. It is in this intimate circle that we are most "ourselves," where our jokes are best appreciated, our special dishes most enjoyed. These are the people to whom we go first when we need comfort or empathy, for they speak our own brand of cultural shorthand, and always know the correct things to say, the proper things to do.

Clambake provides an insider's view into just such a world, that of the contemporary Wampanoag people. If we are ourselves Wampanoag, we will probably nod often while reading these pages, affirming the familiar, approving that this tribal family keeps alive and passes on the traditional way to host an *appanaug*, or clambake. If we belong to another tribe, we will follow this special journey of initiation and education with interest, gaining respect for a way of doing things that's rich and rewarding.

This is a book about people who are neither exotic nor unusual. If you encountered them at a shopping mall or at a movie theater they might seem at first glance like anyone else, a grandfather proud of his grandson, American as apple pie. *Clambake* does not dispute this picture, but it does expand it.

Michael Dorris is the author of *A Yellow Raft in Blue Water, The Broken Cord,* and, with Louise Erdrich, *The Crown of Columbus.* His first book for children is *Morning Girl.*

Steven Peters is a Wampanoag Indian. He lives in Plymouth, Massachusetts, the town where the Pilgrims landed in 1620. Steven is 12 years old and in sixth grade at the Plymouth-Carver Intermediate School. He gets pretty good grades, but his mother thinks they could be better. Steven loves to play sports, especially soccer, baseball, and football, as well as video games such as Nintendo. Steven lives with his mother, Paula, his stepfather, Peter, and his baby sister, Rhiannon.

Plymouth is about 20 miles from Mashpee, a town on Cape Cod. Wampanoag people have lived in Mashpee and other parts of southeastern Massachusetts for many centuries. Wampanoag is an Algonquian word that means "people of the first light." Like most of the Indian tribes in the eastern part of North America, the Wampanoags spoke a dialect, or variation, of the Algonquian language.

The Wampanoags' home, Mashpee, lies on Cape Cod, a peninsula that curls out from the southeastern tip of Massachusetts.

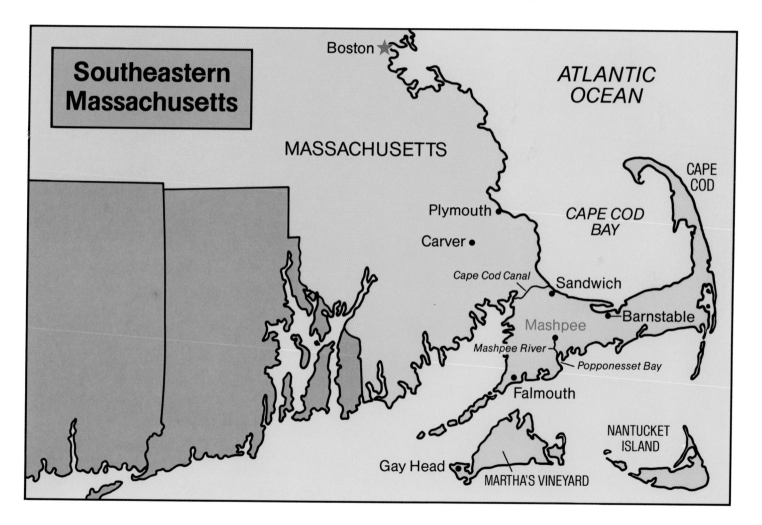

Steven always looks forward to visiting his relatives who live in Mashpee. He and his grandfather fish for herring in the Mashpee River and for clams, oysters, and quahogs at Popponesset Bay. Steven feels lucky because his grandfather, Fast Turtle, believes in keeping the old ways alive. He wants to teach Steven about Wampanoag culture as Steven grows up in modern America. When Steven was a young boy, the tribe's medicine man gave him the name Red Mink.

As the warmest months of the summer approached this year, Fast Turtle decided it was time to introduce Steven to a special Wampanoag tradition, the appanaug. *Appanaug* means "seafood cooking" or "clambake." An appanaug is a ceremony that celebrates a change in season or honors an important person in the tribe. Nonnative people on Cape Cod and in New England also hold clambakes, but these are not ceremonies— they are usually social occasions, something like a barbeque. A Wampanoag clambake involves much preparation and a special way of making the food.

Fast Turtle has taught Steven a lot about fishing. Now he wants to show Steven how to put on a clambake.

Grandfather suggested that they hold the appanaug in July, during the full moon. The shellfish would be plentiful then, and the lobsters would swim close to the shore. This appanaug would honor Hazel Oakley, an elder of the tribe. Steven and Fast Turtle invited many family members and friends.

Fast Turtle told Steven that it would take a lot of hard work to get ready for the appanaug—it was a big responsibility. Fast Turtle learned how to prepare an appanaug from his father, who had learned from his father before him. In turn, Grandfather said, Steven would pass the tradition on to his own children.

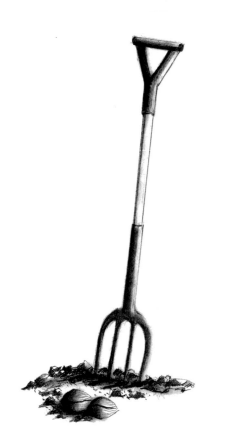

Some of the preparations for the clambake, such as gathering the rocks and wood for the fire, could be done the day before the ceremony. To cook the seafood, rocks would be heated, then the food placed on the hot rocks. Only a certain kind of rock is used in a clambake. Fast Turtle took Steven to Popponesset Bay and showed him where to find the "rock people"—the stones that would be used to heat the food. In the Wampanoag view of the world, everything has a spirit, including rocks and trees.

As they walked over to Punkhorn Point, a peninsula that sticks out into Popponesset Bay, Steven could smell the salt air and the rich, dark mud of the bottom of the bay. A channel flowing from the Mashpee River to the bay separates Punkhorn Point from a small, uninhabited island named Gooseberry Island. This channel was a great spot for digging clams. The moon would be full the next day, and the tides would be lower. When the tide is low, the water recedes from the shore, exposing more of the bay bottom. Grandfather gestured toward the high-tide mark. "This is where we'll get the shellfish tomorrow," he said. "But in the meantime, let's get the rocks."

Steven and Fast Turtle wade in the warm water of the bay.

Steven loved Popponesset Bay because it was so peaceful. The only sounds were the wind, the seagulls, and the soft lapping of the waves on the shore. Steven could almost sense his ancestors' presence as he and his grandfather walked along the water's edge.

They waded into the water and came to a place where they found many rocks that were just the right size, about 10 to 12 inches around. The gentle force of the tide washing over them for many years had worn them smooth. Fast Turtle and Steven carried many heavy stones across the marsh to the spot where the clambake was to be held.

Grandfather, who was going to be the "bakemaster" of the appanaug, had chosen the location for the ceremony by walking in the woods until he had a good feeling that he had found the right place. The spot he picked was in the middle of the forest, away from the noise and traffic of town.

First Steven digs a shallow pit in the ground, then he and his grand-father will arrange the rocks in it.

Grandfather showed Steven how to arrange the stones. First he drew a large oval around the stick he had used to mark the clambake spot. Then he told Steven to dig a shallow pit with a shovel. Finally Steven and Grandfather carefully laid the rocks in the pit so that they formed a pile that was even with the surface of the ground.

Steven noticed that the oblong shape of the pit seemed to have a special meaning. "It's like the 'circle of life' that the medicine man told us about," he said.

Grandfather agreed. "We're carrying on a tradition that our ancestors gave us." He added, "We just have one more task before we call it quits for the day." They walked through the forest and gathered dry wood, which would be used to heat the rocks. Soon they had piled lots of wood next to the clambake pit.

"That's enough for one day —let's go home and get some rest. Tomorrow is a big day," Grandfather said.

Even though Steven was tired, he could hardly sleep that night. He told his mother, "I can't wait for the clambake!" When he finally fell asleep, he dreamed about the rocks and the fire.

Steven's ancestors inhabited Mashpee long before the English landed on Cape Cod in 1620. In those times, the Wampanoags were hunters and gatherers. They planted corn, beans, and squash in the spring and harvested the crops in the late summer and fall. In the winter, the Wampanoags hunted deer, bear, rabbit, and wild turkey. And, in the spring and summer, they took shellfish and finfish from the rivers and bays. As the seasons changed, the Wampanoags gave thanks to the Great Spirit for the many gifts that each new season brought.

Beginning in the early 1600s, Europeans moved to the land where the Wampanoags and other Native Americans lived. The English colonists named the towns they built after places in their old country—Plimouth (now spelled Plymouth), Carver, Sandwich, Falmouth, and Barnstable.

After the Europeans arrived, the Wampanoags continued to hunt and fish and maintain their way of life. They practiced their own religion, which included a respect for the earth and all the living beings on it. The Wampanoags passed their customs and history from one generation to the next by word of mouth.

Over time, however, the Wampanoag way of life changed. The tribe lost most of its land in Mashpee. Many roads, houses, towns, and shopping centers were built. Deer no longer roam the forests, because most of the wooded areas have been cleared. Expensive homes now sit on much of the land along the bay where the Wampanoags dug clams and quahogs. The water of the bays and rivers is getting polluted. These changes have forced the Wampanoag people to work harder to maintain their tribal culture.

The headquarters of the Wampanoag tribe is in Mashpee.

Steven is worried about pollution and would like to work to preserve the environment. One of the Wampanoags' beliefs is that each generation is responsible for keeping the land clean and safe for the next seven generations. Steven's grandfather has talked with him about ways that he can do his part to respect the earth.

The morning of the clambake, Steven awoke at the crack of dawn. He jumped out of bed and put on his shorts. If he hurried, the tide would be low just in time for him to dig the clams. When he arrived at Popponesset Bay, the tide was still going out and the water wasn't quite low enough yet. He decided to get the quahogs first. A quahog is a hard-shelled clam. For the appanaug, the quahog's juice is saved and its meat is chopped into small chunks. Then the juice and meat are cooked together into a chowder.

Opposite: *Nebosett and Mishanagqus join Steven to help collect quahogs.* Above: *Steven invites them to come into the water with him. Part of the fun of gathering quahogs is splashing around in the water.*

Just as Steven was about to wade into the bay, his friend Mishanagqus and her cousin Nebosett came into the clearing and asked him what was going on. Steven told them that he was preparing a clambake.

"Can we help?" they asked.

"Sure, come on. We need a basketful of quahogs so my mother can make the chowder," Steven said.

23

The three friends show off their quahogs.

Steven waded into the water and felt around on the bottom of the bay with his feet the way his grandfather had taught him. When his foot touched something that felt like a small rock, he reached down into the mud to pull up the quahog. Sometimes it wasn't a quahog, but a rock. If it was a rock, he threw it out into the deep part of the bay so that he would not be tricked again—at least not by that rock. The three friends fished around in the water, and before long they had filled a large basket with quahogs, enough for a chowder to satisfy all the guests. They set the quahogs onshore under a pine tree to keep them cool.

24

Left: *Steven gives his mother the quahogs he and his friends collected for her chowder.* Below: *An airhole usually means that there are clams underneath.*

Next on the list of things to do was the digging of the other clams, the sickissuogs. *Sickissuog* means "clam that spits." These soft-shelled clams squirt saltwater as they are taken from their sandy homes. Fast Turtle had taught Steven to dig at the edge of the bay for sickissuogs. Now that the tide was low, the timing was perfect.

Steven showed Mishanagqus and Nebosett how to look for the telltale air holes in the sand, a sign that a clam was underneath. When they saw a small geyser of water shoot out of one of the holes, Steven shouted excitedly, "There they are—let's get 'em!"

Using a pitchfork, Steven and his friends dug in the sand. When the fork had gone down a few inches, the snout of a clam appeared. As Steven scooped the clam out of the sand, it suddenly squirted a spray of salty water into his face. "No wonder they are called sickissuog," Steven said. They all laughed.

There's time for a quick swim before washing the freshly dug clams.

Soon Steven, Mishanagqus, and Nebosett had dug holes all over the bay and had collected a large basketful of the clams. The children washed them carefully to get as much of the sand out as possible. They finished just in time because the tide had begun to come back in and water was filling the holes they had made.

27

Bubbles filled with saltwater grow on the leaves of rockweed.

Now it was time to begin the next task—gathering the rockweed. This greenish-brown, rubbery seaweed is placed over the rocks during a clambake to protect the food from being scorched by the hot rocks. The plant has bubbles on it that are filled with salty water. The saltwater heats up and steams the food, giving it a naturally salty taste. Rockweed can be found all over Popponesset Bay, clinging to rocks and mussels. Steven's grandfather came to help him gather the rockweed. They placed it in neat piles near the clambake pit.

Grandfather pulled Steven aside to tell him what a good job he had done so far. "If you keep this up, we're going to have a great appanaug," he said. They were just about ready to start the clambake. "This is where everything comes together," Fast Turtle told Steven.

John Peters, the Wampanoag medicine man, and Ellsworth Oakley, the supreme sachem

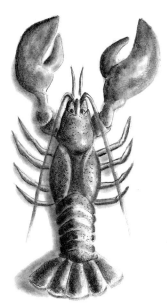

*T*he guests began to arrive for the clambake. First came Slow Turtle, the medicine man of the Wampanoag, also known as John Peters. The medicine man is the Wampanoag spiritual leader. He presides over weddings, naming ceremonies, funerals, and tribal ceremonies. Then came Drifting Goose, or Ellsworth Oakley, the supreme sachem. The sachem guides the tribe in its relations with other Indian nations. Finally some elders and their children and grandchildren arrived. Hazel Oakley, the guest of honor, came with her two grandchildren.

The sky darkened, and rain began to fall. Steven was afraid that the festivities would be spoiled by the rain. Just then, Slow Turtle raised his arms to the sky and murmured a prayer. To Steven's amazement, the rain stopped and the sun came out. Slow Turtle said with satisfaction, "Let the appanaug begin."

The guests all helped get everything ready. For the clambake to be ready to eat at 2:00 P.M., the fire had to be lit at 11:00 A.M. It would burn until about 1:00 P.M. Then, when the rocks were scorching hot, the food would be placed on them to cook for an hour.

Grandfather showed Steven how to arrange the wood over the rocks and start a fire. Soon the fire was blazing. Some of the guests worked to keep the fire going. They raked the burning wood so that the hot ashes fell into the crevices of the rocks. The ashes enveloped the rocks, heating them through.

As the rocks were heating, Grandfather and Steven checked to make sure that there was plenty of wood for the fire and enough food for all the guests. Everything was ready. The clams that Steven, Mishanagqus, and Nebosett had dug that morning were clean and ready to cook. The chowder was simmering on the stove. Steven's mother had wrapped corn on the cob, potatoes, onions, and spicy sausage in individual cheesecloth packets to be placed on the rocks. And there were enough lobsters for everyone. They were of good size, almost two pounds each. Fast Turtle had bought the fresh lobsters at a lobster market in Sandwich, on the Cape Cod Canal.

Fast Turtle and his niece Ramona carry the food to the bake bed.

Left: *Fast Turtle, the bakemaster, gets the clams ready to be put on the fire.* Below: *Corn, potatoes, onions, and sausage are wrapped in packets.*

Grandfather said that the clambake was going according to schedule. About 25 friends and tribal elders had arrived, and excitement was building. The people were eager to celebrate the first feast of the summer, and to honor Hazel Oakley for her service to the tribe.

33

Steven and some of the guests began to place rockweed on the hot rocks. The mussels that were still hanging on the rockweed would cook with the rest of the food and be part of the appanaug. As the rockweed touched the rocks, it sizzled and hissed. Steam rose up and the sharp smell of salt filled the air.

Then came the magic moment when Steven, under the watchful eye of Fast Turtle, placed the food on the steaming rockweed. First came the packets of corn, potatoes, onions, and sausage, which Steven and his friends spread evenly over the surface of the clambake bed. Next they laid the clams on the bake. Finally they put the squirming lobsters on top of the pile of food. The live lobsters tried to get away, but they stopped moving as the heat of the hot rocks began to bake them.

When all the food was on the bake bed, Steven and his friends topped it with more rockweed and a plastic cover to keep in the steam. Some of the steam seeped from under the cover, and the salty, mouth-watering smell of the clambake wafted through the air.

Mishanagqus and Steven drop handfuls of rockweed onto the hot rocks.

Steam rises up around the food. Inset: After all the food is on the bake bed, a plastic cover is placed over the whole thing.

Left: *John Peters, known as Slow Turtle.* Below: *Hazel Oakley's granddaughter Annette.* Opposite: *The elders of the tribe tell the young people about the Wampanoags' history.*

The clearing was very quiet now. Slow Turtle raised his arms to the sun and offered a prayer to the Great Spirit. When he finished the prayer, he asked the guests to hold hands and form a circle. He spoke of the value of all living things, the winged creatures, the animals that walk the forests, the finfish, the shellfish, and the plants and trees. He also thanked the Great Spirit for the morning rain, which had cleansed the earth and watered the trees and plants.

"May the Great Spirit protect us, keep us together, and keep our love for Mother Earth," he said. As he finished speaking, the guests said "Ho," the Wampanoag way of saying "Amen." Under the guidance of the tribal leader, all the guests silently gave their thanks to the Great Spirit.

The sound of a drum broke the silence, followed by a flute. The guests in the circle began to dance. They danced clockwise to thank the good spirits and counterclockwise to pay respect to the evil spirits.

38

Drifting Goose reminded the guests that this clambake was being held in honor of Hazel Oakley, in appreciation for her many years of service to the members of the tribe. He turned to Hazel and thanked her. Then the medicine man and the supreme sachem asked Red Mink and his grandfather to come to the center of the circle. The medicine man praised Fast Turtle for passing on the Wampanoag traditions to Red Mink. Red Mink was asked to say a few words. He was very proud, but all he could think of was the hard work that had gone into the clambake. He blurted out, "The chowder is ready!"

Hazel Oakley, the guest of honor

The chowder is served!

A murmur of approval came from the guests, and they all lined up to get a bowl of the delicious quahog chowder that Steven's mother had prepared. The chowder sharpened their taste buds for the clambake. Soon the appanaug would be ready to serve.

As everyone was finishing off the chowder, Steven and his grandfather announced that the time had come to uncover the main attraction. The guests circled the clambake and watched as Fast Turtle carefully lifted the cover from the baked seafood and vegetables. The top layers of rockweed were removed, exposing the bright red lobsters. The clams and mussels were open, ready to be eaten, and the potatoes, corn, and onions were steaming in their packets.

Steven enlisted the help of some of the guests to serve the food. Every plate was filled with lobsters, clams, vegetables, and sausage. After all the guests were served, Steven and Grandfather got a chance to taste the rewards of their labor. Everything was delicious. Steven cleaned his plate.

Steven and his grandfather fill the guests' plates with the tasty food.

43

Drifting Goose complimented Red Mink, Mishanagqus, and Nebosett for their efforts. He stressed the importance of the oral tradition—the Wampanoag way of passing on knowledge by word of mouth, like the way Fast Turtle had taught Red Mink about the appanaug. Drifting Goose then gave Red Mink an eagle feather. This gift was something he would be proud to wear at Indian events.

As the sun set in the western sky, Steven turned to his grandfather. "Thanks, PaPa, I'll never forget this," he said.

Slow Turtle talks to Steven about the eagle feather he received.

It had been a long day, and now it was time for Steven to go home to Plymouth. He wanted to get a good night's sleep, because his baseball team was playing the Kingston Giants the next day.

"Now that I know how to do a clambake," Steven said, "maybe I could put one on for my team at the end of the season."

Grandfather smiled. "That would be nice. I'm sure you will make a good appanaug."

45

Word List

Algonquian—American Indian people from the northeastern and north-central United States and east-central Canada; many tribes, including the Wampanoag, Abenaki, Iroquois, Huron, and Ojibway are part of the Algonquian language and culture group. Algonquian people speak dialects of the language that is also referred to as Algonquian.

appanaug—an Algonquian word that means "seafood cooking"; it is used to mark a change in season or honor someone in the tribe

bakemaster—the person in charge of the appanaug

medicine man—a traditional tribal spiritual leader

mussel—a dark-shelled mollusk, or shellfish

quahog—a hard-shelled clam; depending on their size, the clams are called (from smallest to largest) littlenecks, cherrystones, necks, and bull quahogs

rockweed—a greenish-brown seaweed that attaches to rocks and mussels

sachem—a traditional tribal leader who is responsible for the government and the welfare of the people

sickissuog—a soft-shelled clam that squirts water

Wampanoag—American Indian people from southeastern Massachusetts; the word means "people of the first light," or "people of the dawn"

Pronunciation Guide

appanaug—APP-uh-nawg

Mishanaqgus—mish-AWN-uh-gus

Nebosett—nuh-BOSS-et

Popponesset—POPP-uh-nes-ut

quahog—KWOH-hog

sachem—SAY-chum

sickissuog—SICK-ih-sahg

Wampanoag—WOMP-uh-NO-ag

For Further Reading

Coombs, Linda. *Powwow.* Cleveland, OH: Modern Curriculum Press, Inc., 1991.

Cwiklik, Robert. Intro. by Alvin M. Josephy, Jr. *King Philip and the War with the Colonists.* Englewood Cliffs, NJ: Silver Burdett, 1989.

Jennings, Paulla. *Strawberry Thanksgiving.* Cleveland, OH: Modern Curriculum Press, Inc., 1991.

Lester, Joan A. *We're Still Here: Art of New England/The Children's Museum Collection.* Boston: The Children's Museum, 1987.

Peters, Russell M. *The Wampanoags of Mashpee.* Barnstable, MA: The Indian Spiritual and Cultural Council, 1987.

Rothaus, James. *Squanto: The Indian Who Saved the Pilgrims.* Mankato, MN: Creative Education, 1988.

Sewall, Marcia. *People of the Breaking Day.* New York: Atheneum, 1990.

Weinstein-Farson, Laurie. Frank W. Porter III, gen. ed. *The Wampanoag.* New York: Chelsea House Pub., 1989.

Ziner, Feenie. *Squanto.* Hamden, CT: Linnet Books, 1988.

About the Contributors

Russell M. Peters is a Mashpee Wampanoag of the Turtle Clan. His Indian name is Fast Turtle. Growing up in Mashpee, Massachusetts, Peters attended a three-room school. After graduation, he joined the U.S. Army and served five years of active duty. His education includes a B.S. degree in Business Administration from Morgan College in Baltimore, Maryland, an M.Ed. from Harvard University, and a fellowship in Urban Studies and Planning from the Massachusetts Institute of Technology. After working for 14 years in the computer industry, Peters went to work with the Coalition of Eastern Native Americans. In 1974, he became president of the Mashpee Wampanoag Indian Tribal Council and was involved in the tribe's attempt to recover ancestral lands. Peters is the author of *The Wampanoags of Mashpee,* a historical portrait of the tribe from 1620 to the present. He also served as project director of "People of the First Light," a series of films about New England Native American tribes. The programs were broadcast on public television. Peters lives in Jamaica Plain, Massachusetts. He has six children and seven grandchildren.

John Madama is a photographer, writer, and desktop publisher. He owns North Atlantic Graphics and teaches computer publishing and visual design at Harvard University, the Massachusetts Institute of Technology, and Radcliffe College. He holds a B.S. degree in Microbiology with a minor in Art History from Rutgers University and was a fellow in Environmental Planning at Tufts University. He has worked as a designer, editor, video producer, and photographer on many projects involving Native Americans, science, and the environment. John's home and studio is located on Rocky Neck—the oldest working art colony in the country—in Gloucester, Massachusetts.

Series Consultant **W. Roger Buffalohead**, Ponca, has been involved in Indian Education for more than 20 years, serving as a national consultant on issues of Indian curricula and tribal development. He holds a B.A. in American History from Oklahoma State University and an M.A. from the University of Wisconsin, Madison. Buffalohead has taught at the University of Cincinnati, the University of California, Los Angeles, and the University of Minnesota, where he was director of the American Indian Learning and Resources Center from 1986 to 1991. Currently he teaches at the American Indian Arts Institute in Santa Fe, New Mexico. Among his many activities, Buffalohead is a founding board member of the National Indian Education Association and a member of the Cultural Concerns Committee of the National Conference of American Indians. He lives in Santa Fe.

Series Consultant **Juanita G. Corbine Espinosa**, Dakota/Ojibway, serves as director of Native Arts Circle, Minnesota's first statewide Native American arts agency. She is first and foremost a community organizer, active in a broad range of issues, many of which are related to the importance of art in community life. In addition, she is a board member of the Minneapolis American Indian Center and an advisory member of the Minnesota State Arts Board's Cultural Pluralism Task Force. She was one of the first people to receive the state's McKnight Human Service Award. She lives in Minneapolis.